Dad of Ed

By

Jeff Barnhill

TABLE OF CONTENTS

WHY A BOOK?

STOP!! Before you read anymore, please make sure you are not reading this to learn how to cope with a loved one with an eating disorder, as a father. **DO NOT** read any further, find your loved one a doctor, therapist, psychologist and most importantly a dietitian that understands patients with an eating disorder. Hopefully, you are not at the point of inpatient rehab, but don't waste time. Listen to the professionals and act fast. If you let this illness go, you could be facing a long, long road to recovery.

Why a book? I don't know, maybe too much time on my hands. No, the reason is if you go to the local bookstore or your online book outlets you will find plenty of books written by recovered or recovering patients of Eating

Disorders. You will also find books written by parents, mainly by moms who write their painful memories. However, you will very rarely find a book written by the dad. Dads are more than the money cow who pays for the treatment, and who makes the decisions of how treatment and recovery goes. Frankly, it's quite the opposite. I found that the role of dad was the human punching bag. I did have to fork up the money, which was fine with me, I just wanted a healthy daughter, I did have to find a facility to take our daughter to, and I did have to take the punches from the questions from the emotional mother who doesn't understand how this could be happening to us. I am not a hero and I am not writing this book to get pats on the back. I am simply writing this book because I wanted to give people a look into what it looked like from a father's view. This is not to say this is how every dad will see the eating disorder process, nor am I saying this is a book about what to do or don't. Probably, it may be more of the Don'ts by the time I get finished.

Go ahead and have the pity party and woe is me time. But remember to make this time short and move toward the recovery process. There will be plenty of time for these parties of self-reflection and the non-understanding portion of this disease. Also, if you don't have friends or loved ones that have dealt with this before, be patient. They are going to make stupid comments and ask questions you are still asking yourself. Are you kidding me? The one comment that I still get today that just drives me crazy is, "why don't you just put the food in front of her and make her eat it." Well, crap, I should have given you the money it took for rehab and all would have been great. Horse dung, it's really not that simple.

The other important topic you need to understand is that this issue is NOT your fault. It is oh so easy to find excuses that will make you feel that in some way you or your spouse had something to cause this eating disorder. I can tell you that I am a big boy and mom is not the smallest of women out there. So, looking at this, did she look at us and tell herself that she wasn't going to grow up and look like us? This took the longest for me to understand. It was finally during a family week during her treatment the director of the treatment facility told every family to take that burden off your backs and move forward. I can tell you that to this day our daughter still claims it had nothing to do with our outward appearance.

We are like most families, a dad and mother that works, and two beautiful children. Mom had to quit work after treatment to stay home with our daughter to make sure the recovery process is moving in the best and right direction. God blessed our family with a beautiful little (no pun intended) girl and a handsome little boy, 22 months apart. Both mom and dad grew up in eastern North Carolina for most of our lives and now call Arkansas home.

Insurance. You may be asking yourself why I am discussing insurance. During the course of our daughter's treatment my wife and I got to see so many girls that have to leave the facility before they were completely ready to return home. Based on the treatment team conversations, most of these girls return within a few weeks. So, find out what your insurance will cover and work very diligently to get confirmation that the insurance company will cover the total treatment. This is all I am going to dive into this topic, as we have great insurance, but I am no expert on how this process would work if you needed to have those difficult conversations. The only advice I have is to tell the insurance company that they can pay for it now or pay for it later, because like I said, most girls who are forced out are repeat patients.

THE CALM BEFORE THE STORM

The calm before the storm is a reference to my life living in costal eastern NC. Hurricanes were almost guaranteed each year. Right before a hurricane made landfall the weather would change. The wind would stop blowing and most times the day was sunny and just a beautiful day. Hence, the calm before the storm.

I remember the day when the arguments around bathroom time became the everyday occurrence. I would come home from work and hear the battle between my wife and daughter over how long she had been in the bathroom. Music in the background, I would assume at the time, a girl who is going through her teenage years.

(Remember, the hospital didn't give us parents an owner's manual when we brought the bundles of joy into this world.) The door locked and the screaming that my stomach hurts or I'm pooping.

Having nightly conversations between my wife and me about something isn't right. Never, I mean never, did the words of eating disorder come out of our mouths. She was way too smart and beautiful to be starving herself or forcing herself to vomit. In the weeks to come, the bathroom visits became worse and worse. School became a battle every morning. Strange, being that our daughter is a social butterfly. I realize this was her teenage years and I guess life is different than it was when I was a young adult but, please.

The day finally came when the bathroom visits began to be more frequent and more noticeable that she really had an intestinal issue. Every time she would eat it wasn't long before she was running to the restroom to either to have explosive diarrhea or vomiting. The decision was made; she was going to see our family physician. The decision was made to check her gallbladder. Guess what, her gallbladder was not functioning, causing the intestinal issues. Whew, problem solved. Surgery, and we would be back to normal. Surgery day came and we went home and she stayed away from greasy foods (doctor's orders). Not only did she stay away from greasy foods she stayed away from any food that made her sick during the diagnostic process with the gallbladder. All of a sudden our daughter had basically become a vegetarian.

Let's back up and let me give you an overview of what dad does for a living. Dad is a production manager for a protein company that produces chicken, pork and beef. I myself am on the live side of pork production. So, when you have a daughter that tells you that she didn't want to eat meat anymore, you can imagine, this was a little shocking and unexpected. We are talking about a kid who grew up eating liver pudding like candy. Liver pudding is a southern dish that is what the name says it is. I'll let you do the research to understand the nature of liver pudding. After doing your homework, you will realize that if a child would eat it, and loved it, you will understand why it was strange that she only wanted bland foods.

THE TRUTH CAN HURT SOMETIMES

After watching our daughter continue to battle the recovery process from the gallbladder issue we watched her start to rapidly lose weight. We just thought that this was the aftermath of the gallbladder surgery. This is when the lies, manipulation and misleading began.

She was now telling us and the doctor that she wasn't able to use the restroom and laxatives were given as a treatment method. Wow, how stupid could we have been? Remember, this is where the lies began. So, laxatives became a normal treatment program in which reality was feeding the eating disorder.

One night my wife and I were lying in bed and we began to talk out loud about the chances that our daughter might have an eating disorder. However, as parents you want to give your children the best opportunity to be truthful and tell you when life is having its struggles. Finally, my wife found a therapist in our local area for our daughter to see once a week.

After several sessions with the therapist, our daughter finally admitted she thought she had an eating disorder and didn't know how to cope or avoid the voices that the eating disorder "Ed" was telling her to do. Ed by this time had complete control of her life and we were just sitting around thinking we were doing the best for our daughter. During this time she was seeing her regular family physician and the therapist. We found a dietitian in the nearby town, but realized quickly that they were not experienced enough to deal with eating disorder patients.

Our daughter starting exhibiting seizure type episodes and everyone was in agreement that this was being caused by the low blood sugar. I will dive deeper into this later on. The seizures were very scary and seemed to happen each night. It finally got to the point that she was sleeping with an air horn that she could use when she felt a seizure coming on.

This is when the truth hurts. I came home one afternoon the week before Thanksgiving and was met at the door by our daughter. She asked if we could talk. Now, those of you who have a teenage daughter the first thing that popped into my mind was that she was pregnant. I can remember saying "if you are pregnant we need to get her mother before we continue this conversation." She relieved my mind when she said, no, this is not what she wanted to talk to me about. Now, my mind was racing with what she could say that was this important. She calmly stated that she appreciated everything we had done to help her get over her eating disorder, but local treatment was not working as well as she had wished for. My reaction and question was "what are you trying to tell me?" I want to go to a rehabilitation facility and get my life back. A fifteen girl just told her family that she wanted to go away and kick Ed's a@%. I couldn't imagine how scared she must have been to drop that news in our laps without any pre-warning. Do you know how mature and how responsible that sentence really meant? I asked if she had thought this through and that she would be away from home for several months and her response was "I won't be here in a few months if I don't."

So, the next morning I started looking for local rehab centers. There were plenty of psychological facilities, but none in our area that treated eating disorders specifically. Don't get me wrong, an eating disorder is a psychological disorder, but we needed somewhere they strictly treated eating disorder patients. After about two hours into my search I ran across a facility that was roughly an hour and a half away. Not ideal, but they had great reviews.

I picked up the phone and called the facility and gave them our story and they said they would have a room the first of the year. This was a month and a half away. We immediately began to gather all the paperwork and visiting our family physician on a bi-weekly basis to monitor her health. The seizures became worse and her activity level dropped to her basically being able to just lie around the house. Any extra activities would completely exhaust all of her energy reserves and would keep her in bed most of the next day. Her body had basically gone into hibernation. Her heart had got to the point where it was working just enough to keep the vital organs working and that was it. In my mind looking back at it, she was one shock or scare away from having a heart attack.

HAPPY NEW YEAR

On Monday, January 4th we loaded up and headed toward the treatment facility. Our daughter lay in the back seat and slept all the way there. Good news about that was if she tried to escape, she wouldn't have a clue where to go because she was totally lost.

We were greeted at the door with a luggage cart and up the elevator we went. They took our daughter off to meet with her treatment team and left us in a room to sign her life away. Believe me, this wasn't their first rodeo. They kept us separated most of the day until it was finally time for us to leave. They gave us fifteen minutes to say our good-byes and at the end of our allotted time the nurse came out and rolled her off to the unit and we left.

One would think the trip home would be a crying fest but in all reality, I felt as if a huge burden had been lifted off my back. My wife just rode in silence. I knew then that this was going to be a rough couple of months.

The next few days seemed very weird not to have her around as this had been the longest she had been away from us and knowing this had to be rough on her as well. Our only time to visit was once a night for ten minutes via phone conversations. Hearing her sad voice was overwhelming. Had we made the right decision was a constant question. The other times to visit were on Saturday and Sunday from 1-5 PM.

Our son went with us the first weekend and quickly realized that just Saturdays would be adequate enough for him. All our daughter wanted to do when we visited was sit in her room and just hang out. Having a 13 year old boy sitting still for 4 hours a day was way too much for him to handle. So after the first weekend the whole family would go on Saturday, and Sunday was a girl's day. They would do nails, wash hair, and do laundry.

FIRST IMPRESSIONS

Logic would tell you that you never get a second chance to make a first impression. Well, I can prove that statement wrong. The day we checked our daughter into rehab we had a private conversation with the director of the facility, who is the head psychologist. What a prick!! He spent fifteen minutes telling us all the research and speeches he gives around eating disorders. Screw that, tell me how you plan on fixing our daughter. I underline the word "fixing" because that was a huge hang up with me during her rehab. There is no fixing an eating disorder. Yep, that's right, there is not a magical pill you take every day and you're healed. I was told very quickly by the treatment team that I had to stop using the term "fixing".

Dr. Todd (name changed due to anonymity) was your typical nerdy looking guy. Very cocky acting in our initial meeting; I checked out mentally after the first five minutes into how great he was. His dialogue was something of a nerd convention and nothing he said made any sense. What have I gotten my daughter into? Dr. Todd came across as having not very good bedside manners what so ever.

Dr. Todd read me like a book; he asked our daughter if I had something against him and if I was that standoffish all the time. She made a casual joke and read me the riot act. From that day forward I made a very conscious effort to get to know him a little better each time we met.

During our first family week at rehab Dr. Todd gave a speech about eating disorders and once again he acted as if he were given a speech to his peer group. Some I understood, but most went right over my head. His approach was strange but all the adolescent patients loved him.

I finally got to know him a little better and ended up thinking he was the best thing since sliced bread. The way he developed relationships with his patients was second to none. Still today we use him as our primary phycologist.

POOH BEAR'S WINTER CAMP

On that chilly, overcast Monday morning we admitted our daughter, with the understanding that she would probably stay for at least three months. Three months, this wasn't the normal week of summer camp; this was like going off to college. Something my wife and I were very fearful of. Even the little brother wasn't so keen on the idea that she was going to be gone for so long. We will talk a bit more about little brother a little later.

From the time our daughter was born, I've always called her Pooh or Pooh Bear. Setting the GPS in my truck was hard enough knowing where we were headed much less type in a name of a psychological facility. So, in an effort to keep everyone in good spirits I used the name

Pooh Bear's Winter Camp. Stupid as it may sound it became a joke every time we got into the truck and had to head that way.

When our daughter arrived, they immediately put her on wheelchair assignment due to her being so malnourished. Wow, was she really in that bad of shape. Makes us feel like wonderful parents let me tell you. Also, due to the seizures she had to wear a bracelet that had "fall risk" printed on it. She kind of thought this was funny due to the fact that she was assigned to a wheelchair, how was she to fall? The wheelchair was to keep her from walking to prevent her from exhausting any calories what so ever. Wheelchair assignment went on for five weeks before she convinced her treatment team that she was eating her meal plans and would ultimately feel part of the group if they allowed her to walk around the unit.

Our daughter had only been in rehab for a week before they had their first family week. Family week was an educational program for families with loved ones in the facility. This is where we as parents learned as much as we could within a week's time about our child's eating disorder.

They brought in a guest speaker in each month for family week. Some girl or lady that had recovered or still recovering so that the patients and parents had a better understanding of what life outside rehab was all about. During this particular guest speaker's speech she began to talk about not being able to go back to her normal life and hang out with her old friends. As soon as this was brought up our daughter began to shake and you could tell her eyes were starting to roll back into her head. I rolled her out into the lobby and within seconds she was lying on the floor having a seizure. Remember, the seizures were diagnosed in the beginning as being brought on by low blood sugar. Low blood sugar at an eating disorder rehab, Hmmm? Eventually, the seizures were finally diagnosed as pseudo seizures being brought on by anxiety. This may sound horrible, but pseudo seizures are seizures that don't send shock waves back into the brain like epileptic seizures do. Epileptic seizures can cause long term brain damage if not monitored or treated with medication.

Once a week we would have a family session with our daughter's therapist. These were done via phone or if we were there for family week we would actually meet in person. Our therapist was a young female who for the sake of keeping names anonymous we will call her Tracy. Tracy and our daughter seemed to hit it off from the very beginning, which was a miracle within itself. They had the same personalities and our daughter loved her. Trusting her and opening up didn't seem to be much of an issue after the first couple of weeks.

Rehab was very structured; they kept the girls busy from the time they woke up to the time they went to bed. Lots of therapy sessions, both group and individual sessions. I could imagine why our daughter didn't adapt very well at first; she is more of on her time personality. However, she seemed to be doing great. Each week we would get a report of her progress and each week she was gaining the appropriate amount of weight, depending on her stage of rehab.

Weight was never discussed, under any circumstances, and neither were calories. Calories were referenced as exchanges. Each patient had their allotted exchanges they had to eat at each meal. I remember someone asking me if our daughter ever got hungry, my answer was quick and honest, NO. They eat six times per day, three meals and three snacks. There wasn't time for them to get hungry.

During our first visit of the full campus, we had the wonderful pleasure to see where our loved one had to meet three times a day for the hardest part of their treatment, the cafeteria. We also had the *great privilege* of meeting the gentleman that was responsible for creating the meals for the patients each and every day. This man was heartwarming and not only did he bring tears to his eyes during his portion of the tour, but he brought tears to every parent there. Chef Luck was a man that looked like one of the Muppet characters by the way he dressed. When he began speaking, it was extremely obvious that he truly felt that his role in the recovery process was one of the most important. To this day I believe he is one of the most important treatment team members. He had the task of scheduling menus that didn't repeat themselves but every thirty days. On top of that, while the patients were not on self-selection he had to portion meals to meet each individual's exchange rate. Also, each patient had the option of making their own menu at the beginning, I guess to help them finish their portions. Can you imagine having to work through this each day of the week? Chef

Luck was as passionate about his role in the recovery process as a parent could have wished for.

Each month they had family week. A three day educational program designed for parents and patients. I was a little optimistic at first but after Dr. Todd's "lecture" the rest was very informative. I give Dr. Todd a lot of crap about his message to parents and seem to be very hard on the man. Believe me when I say, he saved our daughter's life! If it wasn't for Dr. Todd and his staff none of these girls would be in recovery today.

Naming rehab as Winter Camp seemed a little foolish in the beginning, but the longer you were around; it almost had the feeling that it was a camp type atmosphere. As patients would leave, they each had a time where they would sit down with each other and go through a closing session. It was a time for goodbyes and well wishes. Friends were made and some will remain lifelong friends. Even the moms became close and I imagine some will stay in contact for years. During partial treatment, which is a time where the patient is in rehab for six hours a day and spends the rest of the time with a parent (almost all moms), the moms would get together twice a week for a mom session. They talked about what issues they were having with their daughters during this transition period and the struggles they were having. Giving each mom a little to learn about how other parents were dealing with partial treatment and the lessons on how to deal with a teenage girl who has grown so much during her short stay at winter camp.

TABLE TALK

Table talk was a session during family week where the patients would sit down at the table with you (no love ones allowed to be at the same table) and you got to ask questions that you would like to ask your loved one but felt like you couldn't. Also, I think it gave each girl the opportunity to say things at the table that they really wanted their parents to know but were too afraid to tell them. Our first table talk session was just plain weird, I didn't know what to say or ask. I was scared I would say something that would trigger the patient and then I would feel like crap for doing so. This is where I would say God had a plan. We were introduced to three teenage girls who all were very beautiful and intelligent. Again, this seemed to be the common theme at rehab. Every one of the girls was beautiful and smart. It was like this was a prerequisite for becoming a victim of Ed. One young lady captured my heart that day, Denver (again the name changed for anonymity reasons). Denver was a telling it like it is kind of person. She had that little sassiness to her that drew my attention to her for the whole session. She told it like it was and meant every word of it. I remember her telling the group not to take any of the shit that our daughter wanted to give, it was Ed that was saying or doing these things. Be firm but be fair. Denver basically controlled the conversation the whole session. Making it easier on everyone sitting at our table. My heart poured out with emotion for this girl, who could be so brave to sit with a group of strangers and give her life story and help us understand what our daughter was going through but wasn't strong enough yet to kick Ed to the side and move on with life.

The second family week we decided it was time to bring little brother along so that he could get some idea of what his sister was going through. My main goal was to sit at the table talk session with Denver. When that time came I noticed Denver wasn't around. I knew she hadn't been discharged, but where was she? This was the real reason I brought little brother. I later found out that she had gone into refusal and didn't eat for a day. Later that night I asked if I could speak with her, they allowed me to and all that was said was that you are a beautiful and smart individual; don't let this disorder kick your ass. The next morning we got a call from our daughter and she told us that Denver had made up all 30 exchanges last night and was allowed off bed rest. Was it me that convinced her to fight or was it something else? I don't know and really could care less, she fought and is still fighting today, but at her home with family after finishing rehab and being discharged. I wish the very best for Denver and if you are reading this you know who you are and if you ever need anything you know how to find us.

THE HARSH REALITY

So far I think one may be telling themselves this really isn't all that bad. Well, sit back and buckle your seat belt this is where I give you the reality of this disease from my perspective. This disease kicks everyone in the whole family in the butt and takes no prisoners. It doesn't care how old you are, how smart you are, how dedicated you are and who it will affect in the interim. It's not just the person with an eating disorder, it preys upon, it is the whole family. Even the siblings that have nothing to do with this. In some way it is going to alter their life as well.

We watched our daughter waste away for three months before deciding that she truly had an eating disorder. What kind of parent wait that long to get help? Why didn't we pick up on this sooner? How can this be happening to us, we didn't do anything wrong? Yes, these are the questions that run through your mind every single day once you finally realize your sweet little girl has done this to herself. Oh, but wait, she didn't do this to herself, that SOB Ed did! You're right, it seems as if I am a little pissed right now. Well, really I'm not anymore, but I wanted to give you the insight of how I felt for three months. I still struggle from time to time trying to make decisions that are best for our daughter. Does she need to go out with friends; something could trigger her and cause a seizure? If I don't, how is she ever to work herself back into the social scene that she once loved? I could go on for days about the decisions the parents have to make in order to try and do what is best for your loved one, but instead I think you get the point.

Being pissed, now that is how I felt during this whole ordeal. I stayed mad, I tried to keep a smile on my face, but no matter how hard I tried I still couldn't get over the fact that this disease had taken control of our daughter's life. Ed is like the abusive husband that will beat you down either verbally or physically and then talk themselves right back into your life again. You see the black eyes and you see the tears, but you can't convince her that Ed needs to be locked up somewhere and left to rot. No, it doesn't work that way. I really don't know how the therapist works out these issues with patients and teach them the coping skills to keep Ed at a distance. All I do know is that they are very good at what they do.

We all know the toll that an eating disorder takes on the person who is having to deal with this, but what about the friends and family that are around as the support group? Yeah, those that truly care. Ed punishes them also. He takes away their happiness, their free time, their money and the list keeps going. Ed tells your daughter that lying and manipulating her parents are the right thing to do. Telling her that if we bargain with food you can get your way. "Just eat the food and we will go to the bathroom and get rid of it so it doesn't cause you to gain weight." Or, telling the parents that she is going to eat at her friend's house but when she gets there she tells her friend she ate right before coming over. These are just a few of the facts that I know were happening; yes, of course, in hindsight.

Siblings, what is their expected behavior through the treatment and recovery process? How do they participate in a positive manner to show their support? I don't have those answers for everyone, all I know is how Pooh's little brother handled this time. Little brother went about it with the out of sight, out of mind mindset. He figured mom and dad had enough on their plates that he didn't want to put any extra burden or pressure on their shoulders. I applaud him for his courage and maturity, but he was struggling as much as we were. He had day to day issues of being a new teenager and was forcing himself to bottle his problems up and keep those to himself. However, he was smart enough to reach out to someone he really felt comfortable talking to. Ms. Branch (yes, again the name changed for anonymity purposes) is one of the

Jr. High School's guidance counselors. The Lord placed her in our lives for a reason, I know. She visited with little brother just about every day. All the while we hadn't a clue. She invested the time to listen to all the daily fears or difficulties little brother was having. It wasn't until the end of treatment that we determined who was counseling him and words can't express the gratitude for all she has done and the acts she continues to have with little brother.

Little brother struggled more than we thought. He was extremely nervous upon big sisters return home. Also, little brother had his mother taken away from him for two weeks during big sis' partial treatment. This may not sound like a huge issue, but you are talking about a lady that hadn't been away from him for more than three days. Although he and I had tons of fun each afternoon, I wasn't a replacement for his mom. Yeah, did that hurt a little, yes, but I understood. I guess I was a momma's boy growing up also. His worries came out of compassion for her recovery. What were the rules of what he could say or not to say? How did he act during meals? Did he have to walk on eggshells after she came home? All of which a thirteen year old shouldn't have to worry about. Again, an eating disorder didn't care who it punished, it really does punish anyone and everyone involved in the patient's path. Everyone who knows little brother would agree that he is probably the most immature thirteen years old that they have been around. But the same people would agree that once that big sis returned home, he has matured into a great young man. He has done nothing but supported his sister and they seem to have a

better relationship today than they did before she
left.

WELCOME HOME

Finally, Pooh Bear was coming home to the safety and comfort of home. What more could everyone want? All the answered prayers. Life is finally going to be normal again. WHAT?? Normal isn't even in the near future. We all thought that when Pooh got home that life would get back to some type of normalcy and all was going to be great again. Boy were we all wrong.

Life coming home wasn't what I had expected. I thought Pooh would walk in, hug necks and find solitude in the comfort and safe space of her home. Not exactly, I don't know what world I was living in. The treatment team had preached that coming home would take some time and adjustments would be needed. Why, they are coming home!! Watching her was like bringing home a puppy for the first time. The puzzled look in her eyes, the only thing missing was the whimpering that the new puppy makes. I even thought that her redecorated room would be a warm and welcoming sight. Again, wrong. What the heck was going on?

What was missing was the fact that she was now out of the control of professionals and now back where the eating disorder all started. It's kind of like going back to the last bar an alcoholic last got drunk at. That's right, the reference to alcoholism, the relationship between the two are very, very similar. The daily struggle not to take a drink and the daily struggle to eat or not purge. I truly believe the two are very connected. The way both ruin lives and the lives of the loved ones who surround them and the habits. I've never had to be around a loved one who was struggling with alcoholism and pray dearly I never do, but the people who you know who have the stories of recovery are very much similar. As mentioned earlier, the DAILY STRUGGLES, are very much the same. One step at a time, one day at a time and one meal at a time. And there is the bathroom!! That place where all the anxiety began for Pooh and mom. I will never forget the first time Pooh used the restroom in her own home. An announcement was made that she was going to the bathroom and the door left wide open. This was home not rehab. She came out with a giggle and a quick, oops, sorry, I forgot where I was for the moment. The bathroom hasn't been the same since. Yeah, she closes the door, but the lock has been removed also but she still announces that she is going. Give it a minute and the guard dog, mom, and she is standing outside the door asking if everything is alright. At the time of writing this Pooh has been home for three months, hopefully this will get better over time, but all indications lead me to believe we have a long way to go before that happens.

Next was the closet check, making sure all the clothes she left owning was still there? No, most of the jeans where gone and replaced with an appropriate size that she had gotten back to during her rehab. There were a few arguments, but nothing that wasn't easily extinguished. She and her mom came to an agreement that the clothes she had now looked better on her today than the old ones that really made her look sick. Today the closet is full and Pooh seems to be pleased with the outfits that she has and all fit as they should. Getting the wardrobe back in line was almost as expensive as the cost of rehab was (this coming from a dad).

Home is where the heart is, today is much better. She has her days, but for the most part she finds solitude and peace within these four walls. I can tell you that she isn't the same as she was before she became sick, but it is a hell of a lot better than it was prior to her leaving for treatment.

FINAL ADJUSTMENTS

I would like to tell each of you that adjusting to being home was an easy transition but it wasn't. Actually, it was quite difficult. Mom tried so very hard to keep the structure and times of meals the same as they were in rehab, but let's face it, we were trying to move on with our lives. And life doesn't work on your time; it has its own agenda. Trying to keep things on a schedule was hard on mom as it was for everyone else. She takes great pride in keeping the norm the norm. However, it doesn't matter how hard you try to keep a tight schedule something is bound to come up and throw that out the window. So, you do the best you can and eat when you find the time. My suggestion is don't try and keep up with your loved one, you will gain weight immediately. You need to remember you are dealing with a teenager whose metabolism is working a heck of a lot faster than yours is. I tried the first couple of days after Pooh came home to eat with her for every meal and snack. Let's just say Pooh and I came to an agreement that I didn't have to eat every time she did. I'm thankful for that, I am heavy enough as it is.

Today there are fewer arguments over the wellbeing of her and what she is allowed to do and where she can go. We have only allowed her to eat a meal away from home and let me tell you mom about killed me because it was me that gave permission for her to do so. So, to keep out of the dog house I asked that we video chat while she ate at her friend's house, as weird as it was she agreed and all went well. You may be asking, why are you being so weird about her eating away from home? Remember, that trust was lost months ago with all the lying that went on that got her in this position to begin with. I wish I could tell you that life just goes back to normal and they don't try to lie and manipulate you, but they still will, at least we still see these tendencies. Not so much the lying, or at least until today we haven't caught her lying, but the manipulation is around all the time.

Let's talk a bit about the manipulation a little further. Our daughter did and still uses her eating disorder as a manipulation tactic. Why are you continuing to punish me, I've done everything like I have supposed to? Are you going to keep me locked up forever? Why can't I go to this party, I'll be with my supportive friends?

Why? I'll tell you why, you can't go to school because of the anxiety, and you can't stand to be in a public place because you are thinking everyone is judging you and let's not forget what causes your seizure events, ANXIETY. We do these things to protect you, not to punish.

Giving you this information was addressed at the very beginning. This is just my point of view of how we have had to deal with a daughter with an eating disorder. I realize each case will be different. Matter of fact, I know it will. Take what you want from this book and use what you can. Hopefully, I've enlightened you enough to at least prepare you for what might be to come. I can tell you that our case is different, just because we had a fighter on our hands. Let Pooh make up her mind that she wants to do something and the world beware. Not every patient is going to be that determined. Trust me, there were patients in therapy way before we checked in and they are still there today.

I love our daughter with all my heart, which is split two ways. She only gets half of it because little man gets the other. She is a fighter and thank God that is what he has blessed us with. Life has been a struggle and a constantly reminds us that it could be a lot worse. We would drive by the Children's Hospital as we pulled into Pooh Bears Winter Camp and thank God that we weren't having to go there. Children die every day, but prayers and God has given us a second chance at life with our daughter. I just hope and pray that one day she will look back on all this and realize how terrible life was during this time and with that constant reminder keep on the recovery process.

We still weigh her once a week, but she has to stand on the scales backwards so that she can't see what she weighs. By now, I would imagine that if she were allowed to get on the scales on her own she would, at least the first time, get on them backwards.

Meals and snacks are still not as easy as we would like, but she knows she has two choices and those are to get up and eat or we pack and go back to treatment. This comes from Tracy, her inpatient therapist. Tracy's famous line was we do not negotiate with terrorist and the eating disorder is a terrorist. Pooh can't stand that line because she thought I would use it on her every day when she got home. So, that we are all clear on this, I have yet to use this line on her. I have told her to pack her bags because she was going back, and this was because she refused to eat a meal.

If there is one piece of advice I really would like for you to know is, BE STRONG and BE CONSISTENT!! Doing neither of these will allow them to walk all over you and at that point you might as well take them back to therapy. You have lost this game and unless you regroup and come back with a stern message you will continue to lose. I wish every one of you the best and hope your case will be better than ours and you can avoid inpatient treatment all together. There are groups and people out there that have so much experience with eating disorders, you don't have to do this on your own.

EPILOGUE

My understanding of an epilogue is a place
where you needed space to say one last thing.
And this I do! I want to thank EVERYONE
who was on Pooh's treatment team. Without
them Pooh wouldn't be here today. I, also,
would like to thank my wonderful wife whose
only job these days is to keep Pooh on the
correct path of recovery. Bless her heart, thus far
she has been terrific. Also, I couldn't get by
without thanking all the supportive friends and
family members that prayed and cared for Pooh
this whole time and continue to pray and support
her. I would like to thank my employer for
allowing me to attend the parts of treatment that
I felt I needed to be at and they have all have
been extremely supportive. I would like to

thank our treatment team here at home, our family physician and Pooh's therapist. They have been wonderful during our transition back to home. I would like to thank Drizzy (no, this is her real name) Pooh's therapy cat. She has been very good for cuddling with Pooh when she is having a not so good day. Again, my wife, God led me to her to me for some reason, but I know without her none of this would be possible. I wished there were awards for parents that give up everything just to take care of their children, if there were she would have won dozens by now. Sweetheart, I love you to the bottom of the ocean and back. I wish I could show you how much you have meant to our family, but I wouldn't even know where to start to show you our gratitude. And a very, very special thank you to the man upstairs. God, none of this would have been possible without

Your grace and His answering the thousands of prayers he received over the course of all this and the ones he keeps getting.